Sacred Hearts Rising: Finding Your Wings Poems

Within these pages of the Sacred Hearts Book 2 Poems, I hope that you find a 'new light' in which to see your story through another's eyes.

I want to say thank you to each of you for trusting me with your extraordinary stories.

Thank you Colleen Songs, for reading and understanding the stories and creating the beautiful poems for everyone to enjoy.

Much love to all of you - Brenda

Compiler Brenda Hammon - Poems by Colleen Songs

Sacred Hearts Rising: Finding Your Wings Poems

Poems by Colleen Songs for

Authors of Sacred Hearts Rising:

Finding Your Wings

## Table of Contents

1. Encapsulating Darkness...Cowgirl Style –

    Brenda Hammon - 7

2. The Angel Baby -

    Susan Janzen - 9

3. It's Time to Play –

    Jacqueline Carroll - 12

4. D.O.A. –

    Daphne McDonagh - 14

5. Kisses in the Breeze –

    Elizabeth Gagnon - 18

2

Compiler Brenda Hammon - Poems by Colleen
    Songs

Sacred Hearts Rising: Finding Your Wings Poems

6.  That's Life –

    Holly Holmberg - 20

7.  Living Hands –

    Kurtis Clay - 22

8.  Found in Lost –

    Jeanine Le Blanc - 25

9.  Dear Son of Nine –

    Marta Clay - 27

10.  Joy –

    Nancy Nance Chaplin - 29

11.  Dance Me –

    Patricia Dalgleish - 31

12.  My Love –

    Sheree Roughsedge- Agerskov - 33

13.  My Birthday Cake –

    Shey Hennig - 35

Compiler Brenda Hammon - Poems by Colleen
Songs

14. Human. Girl. Woman. Momma –

    Stephanie Leach - 38

15. The Craftsman's Clay –

    Alexis Ellis - 40

16. Tuckin' and Roll –

    Bonnie Nicole - 43

17. The Role –

    Carol Black - 46

18. Beauty Runs Deep –

    Jennifer Strachan - 48

19. The Music Maker –

    Kit Fraser - 51

20. Thank You, Body –

    Laura-Lee Harrison - 53

21. Dear Little Girl, –

    Laureen Nowlan-Card - 55

Compiler Brenda Hammon - Poems by Colleen
Songs

Sacred Hearts Rising: Finding Your Wings Poems

22. Monster, Monster –

    Rachel Dyer - 59

23. Still –

    Rika Harris - 62

24. Trust the Flight -

    Sheryl Rist - 64

25. More For Me (Morphine) -

    Sue Ferreira - 67

26. Scares –

    Tracy Childs - 69

27. Paula, - 71

    Wendy Walsh

28. About Colleen Songs – 73

29 About Brenda Hammon – 76

Compiler Brenda Hammon - Poems by Colleen
Songs

Sacred Hearts Rising: Finding Your Wings Poems

Compiler Brenda Hammon - Poems by Colleen
Songs

## Encapsulating Darkness...Cowgirl Style

*For Brenda Hammon*

I've put you in a holding pen
and tied you by the toe.
The one way out is up or down
there's nowhere else to go.

Your vengeance has no hold on me
in darkness nor in light.
You've wasted your own borrowed life;
a constant will to fight.

You see, I am a Cowgirl now.
no fuss, no muss, no lies.
You had your chance to love so choose,
my horse awaits his ride.

Compiler Brenda Hammon - Poems by Colleen
Songs

Sacred Hearts Rising: Finding Your Wings Poems

I do agree to dis-agree

and send you on your way.

My tears are better left to pine

the sun on rainy, riding days.

Compiler Brenda Hammon - Poems by Colleen
Songs

## The Angel Baby

*For Susan Janzen*


Dear Heavenly Father,


It was You who carried me

through my life's adversities.

I was Your born child first,

birthed to You from him to her.

It was You I felt I had belonged.


At times when I felt lost or lone,

an orphan in my very home,

You kept me singing light

and loved by truth.

 I felt Your wisdom in the air,

like a soft breeze in my hair,

You guided me through stages of my youth.

9

Compiler Brenda Hammon - Poems by Colleen
   Songs

Sacred Hearts Rising: Finding Your Wings Poems

So now I pray to let You know,

from my heart, head, tippy toes,

though I've found him

You're the only one...

who could have filled up his big shoes

that in my mind was just like You,

and as my Father You will always stand.


You see, when he finally arrived

not to me, but by Your side,

it was then all traces I was sent...

to the path where he once walked,

where in mind we've strolled and talked,

and this was how our meeting was sure meant.


T'was You and he who held the door

to that long awaited shore

where I could lay my head

10

Compiler Brenda Hammon - Poems by Colleen
        Songs

and end the roam.

And through the arms of my two brothers,

my two sisters, many others

you held your angel baby,

"Welcome home!"

## It's Time to Play

*For Jacqueline Carroll*


I didn't know I needed you

throughout my grown up years.

You would have saved me from the dark,

gave brave to face my fears.


The time is due to come with me,

I'm ready now to run.

I'm not ashamed to be the girl

who loved the rain and sun.


You may be young and innocent,

some think you may be fooled.

If youth is fresh picked from the vine

Compiler Brenda Hammon - Poems by Colleen Songs

Sacred Hearts Rising: Finding Your Wings Poems

no wiser can be schooled.


Let's talk, let's cry, let's laugh and let

the path that led me rise me.

It's you and me, my little girl

it's time we play and be free.

Compiler Brenda Hammon - Poems by Colleen
Songs

**D.O.A,**

*For Daphne McDonagh*

Spinning and spinning around,

thrashing upon the ground,

cracking the muffled sound,

I am changing,

rearranging.

Feeling no thread of life,

whispering songs of death.

A pool of blood and strife

whirls around me,

I can't find me?

CHORUS:

But. Truth. Will. Find. You.

Sacred Hearts Rising: Finding Your Wings Poems

in Dark. Lit. Places!

Leave. You. Breathless.

Wipes. You. Faceless!

D.O.A!

Past life slips away.

A.O.K.

When living your life

beyond the D.O.A.


I slip back into my shell,

hands fall upon my wound.

A shadow inside the spell,

breathe breaks through the womb.

Wings grow beneath the bed,

carry me till I wake.

Choosing the words I spoke,

Compiler Brenda Hammon - Poems by Colleen
Songs

Sacred Hearts Rising: Finding Your Wings Poems

destiny cures my fate!

CHORUS:

Truth. Will. Find. You.

in Dark. Lit. Places!

Leave. You. Breathless.

Wipes. You Faceless!

D.O.A

Past life slips away.

A.O.K.

When living a life

beyond the D.O.A.


Instrumental solo


*Bridge:*

Dead on Arrival.

Compiler Brenda Hammon - Poems by Colleen
Songs

Sacred Hearts Rising: Finding Your Wings Poems

Life survival.

Bodies spirals.

Sweet revival

D.O.A...A...!

Past life slips away.

A.O.K...A...A...!

I'm living a life

beyond the D.O.A.

I'm living a life

beyond the D.O.A.

Compiler Brenda Hammon - Poems by Colleen
Songs

Sacred Hearts Rising: Finding Your Wings Poems

## Kisses in the Breeze

*For Elizabeth Gagnon*


I was so young and you were gone

before I sang you our first song.

The ones I thought would hold us tight

gave up your ghost in all their fright.


But like a lantern in the dark

you shone a glimmer in my heart.

You lit the walk along this path

and led me to pure love at last.


You and I, now us and them

a family we have always been.

We don't need your skin and bones

Compiler Brenda Hammon - Poems by Colleen
Songs

Sacred Hearts Rising: Finding Your Wings Poems

we've got your spirit in our toes.


Your siblings link this other side,

between dimensions we all ride.

We soar the skies and skim the leaves

and send you kisses in the breeze.

Compiler Brenda Hammon - Poems by Colleen
Songs

## That's Life

*For Holly Holmberg*

Life isn't just a playing field

of roses, grass and fun.

It's full of hurts and gravity

that sets you on your bum.

Living would be boring

if we never shed a tear.

We'd walk around not knowing brave

if never taught to fear.

And fear is more a friend than foe,

puts speed into your pace.

Wallow in its mirk and mire

or sweat to win the race.

And sweating isn't easy

as it comes from force to move.

But each step builds to greatness,

and your purpose needs that groove.

Compiler Brenda Hammon - Poems by Colleen
Songs

## Living Hands

*For Kurtis Clay*

Though I may not look you in the eye,
I feel your heart beat in your sigh.

Touch me not, with mangy sweaters,
but wrap me in soft cotton feathers.

I cannot help when my cup pours forth,
allowing helps me run its course.

Those veggies? Fresh is what I please;
a sautéed dish my tongue does tease.

Most days I feel that I'm not right.
I can't fix this mess it's so 'out of sight!'

Sacred Hearts Rising: Finding Your Wings Poems

I pace and twitch, I can stim some moves.
They help me cope, this urge to groove.

I need step by step to do a task;
My lack of patience? Just a lover's mask.

When I don't feel worthy of this awkward life
I blast the tunes like a butter knife.

Please quiet your child so we both can smile,
and dim the noise so I can stay awhile.

I strive to be all I care to be.
It's chore enough to be me being me.

Build me a day I can spend with joy;
to be clean as a whistle and surprise we avoid.

Compiler Brenda Hammon - Poems by Colleen
Songs

Sacred Hearts Rising: Finding Your Wings Poems

I know I'm a lot to understand,

but thanks to my parents I have living hands.

Compiler Brenda Hammon - Poems by Colleen
Songs

## Found in Lost

*For Jeanine Le Blanc*

Found in lost,

I played with death.

Numbed my mind

in clouds of breath.

I died inside,

I dimmed my life;

a disco ball

of gasping light.


As I grew my wings

you fell away.

You're full of regret,

I've a message to say.

Compiler Brenda Hammon - Poems by Colleen
Songs

That to give you must want,

and to live you must die.

To heal you must hurt,

and to laugh you must cry.

Compiler Brenda Hammon - Poems by Colleen
Songs

## Dear Son of Nine

*For Marta Clay*

Dear Son of nine,

I am so proud of you for opening up the
        dialogue

that moment in Kara's office.

You were brave!

You showed courage

that some grown men could not even muster!

And you were all but nine!

You spoke the words of many.

Too many left unheard and alone.

You led us forward into the awareness

of ancient wisdom;

that we have one mouth to speak

and two ears to listen.

Compiler Brenda Hammon - Poems by Colleen
        Songs

Sacred Hearts Rising: Finding Your Wings Poems

For a reason.

I see you now,

a man who has taken control of his destiny,

built a life using your unique gifts and talents,

and yes, there are still those days;

days when the darkness

comes to remind you

to speak.

And for us to listen.

For you speak.

And for us to simply listen.

I am so proud of you!

Love, Mom.

Compiler Brenda Hammon - Poems by Colleen
Songs

## Joy

*For Nancy Nance Chaplin*

One word can reveal us

a love mantra made.

Layers of letters,

a memory's trade.

Masks carved to figure

the art of one thought.

Hyphens and dashes

give path to life brought.

A vision, an item,

a moment, a name.

Vocals interpret

the image's frame.

Spoken linguistically

Compiler Brenda Hammon - Poems by Colleen
Songs

Sacred Hearts Rising: Finding Your Wings Poems

spun into song,

it just takes one word

to bring home what is gone.

Joy.

## Dance Me

*For Patricia Dalgleish*


Dance me from the morn to dawn.

Dance me in the rain.

Move my feet to dance me where

I need to soften pain.


Dance me in the reflect mirror.

Dance my tears to hope.

Move my heart with life blood's warmth

my chest to rise and float.


Dance me with a lover's lead.

Dance me till I bend.

O'er the lumps and scar's terrain

Sacred Hearts Rising: Finding Your Wings Poems

rocks and fields and sand.

Dance me into ecstasy.

Dance me as I age.

Savour past the wonderland

life's but a playwright's stage.

## My Love

*For Sheree Roughsedge-Agerskov*


I had to walk away, my Love.

I had to set you free.

You carried me too long through life.

I had to find my wings and feet.


You swept me off them years ago.

You wrapped me up in love.

I leaned on you too much, my Dear,

a wingless turtle dove.


I didn't want to see the ground

was too afraid to speak .

You found me then, a bare-souled bird;

Sacred Hearts Rising: Finding Your Wings Poems

a crashing destiny.

I take each step on purpose now,
alone I must exist,
to learn the smile of loving eyes
and blow myself a kiss.

I'm proud because I chose this path
it's more a gift than curse.
I'm overcoming mind and thought
to reap past-lesson's purse.

So when you see me now, my Love
please know I needed you.
You were a song I had to sing
for my life to come true.

Compiler Brenda Hammon - Poems by Colleen
Songs

## My Birthday Cake

*For Shey Hennig*


The sting of rejection burns

no matter the winds of change.

Life passes with twists and turns

yet everything stays the same.


I don't know who you are or why.

I don't know what you even look like.

But when my heart begs to cry

reality sears

the knife in my birthday cake.


I'm loved like a chosen thread

in a family's fabric weave.

Compiler Brenda Hammon - Poems by Colleen Songs

Sacred Hearts Rising: Finding Your Wings Poems

They tell me I'm theirs by choice

and wrap me up in knitted sleeve.


But I still wish I knew you cared.

I wish I had choice to feel.

Wonder if I'd say yes or no

if you came by and asked me

for a piece of my birthday cake.


I know that a person can do

only what they know then is best,

at the time that the choice is met,

the future reveals the mess.


Still I sit here and know I am loved

and conjure up what you're like.

Compiler Brenda Hammon - Poems by Colleen
Songs

Sacred Hearts Rising: Finding Your Wings Poems

Imagining you as the flame

that gave me the life

to light the candle

on my birthday cake.

Compiler Brenda Hammon - Poems by Colleen
Songs

## Human. Girl. Woman. Momma.

*For Stephanie Leach*

Just because you are my Momma
doesn't mean you're not a woman.
You have walked a path of imprints
of your own.

Just because you are a woman
doesn't mean you're more than human.
It means you're much like me:
blood, skin and bones.

Just because you are a human
doesn't mean we're the same version
of the past,
the present,
or the future's cast.

Sacred Hearts Rising: Finding Your Wings Poems

Just because I am your daughter
doesn't mean I have to father
your mistakes, they're yours to make,
though bitter lasts.

The only thing I can do
Is to love you and accept you
as a student on this planet
with me too!

Human. Girl.
And Woman. Momma.
Those agreements we give flaw to,
Right or wrong,
the same as me,
the same as you.

Compiler Brenda Hammon - Poems by Colleen
Songs

## The Craftsman's Clay.

*For Alexis Ellis*

The body I chose

was the wrong one

I suppose,

but without it

I would not have known

who I was

'neath the skin.

You know,

that soul-searching

journey

so many hurry

and long for

but never quite reach

Compiler Brenda Hammon - Poems by Colleen
Songs

Sacred Hearts Rising: Finding Your Wings Poems

in their life time?

But I was blessed

with the choice,

with a voice

and a vice

to work wonders

with-out

and with-in...

Oh, my skin was perfect!

My bones sublime!

My heart,

lungs,

and organs

so very divine!

It was simply the garden

that needed re-tilling,

41

Compiler Brenda Hammon - Poems by Colleen Songs
Compiler Brenda Hammon - Poems by Colleen
Songs

Sacred Hearts Rising: Finding Your Wings Poems

designing,

replanting,

a little snipping,

a little clipping,

a little pruning,

a bit of singing;

the flora of pleasure

refined,

nurtured,

uncovered,

on a potter's carrousel

of wet and wanting

craftsman's clay.

Compiler Brenda Hammon - Poems by Colleen
Songs

## Tuckin' and Roll...

*For Bonnie Nicole*

Out of control,

tuckin' and roll,

I'm gonna break this cycle of life.

Open my eyes,

swallow the fright,

I'm gonna live before I die.

*CHORUS:*

No more vices.

No pointed fingers.

No pain will linger here.

I've jumped off this train

to craft a new chain

each link a happy tear.

Tuckin' and roll.

Compiler Brenda Hammon - Poems by Colleen
Songs

Sacred Hearts Rising: Finding Your Wings Poems

Watching the fight,

scared of the night,

I'm gonna break the shattering glass.

No more abuse,

light up the truth,

I'm gonna rise up from the past.


*CHORUS:*

No more vices.

No pointed fingers.

No pain will linger here.

I've jumped off this train

to craft a new chain

each link a happy tear.

Tuckin' and roll...

Tuckin and roll...

Tuckin and roll...

Tuckin' and roll.

TAG:

Out of control,

tuckin' and roll,

I'm gonna break this cycle of life.

Open my eyes,

swallow the fright,

I'm gonna live before I die.

Tuckin' and roll...

Tuckin and roll...

Tuckin and roll...

Tuckin' and roll.

Compiler Brenda Hammon - Poems by Colleen
Songs

## The Role

*For Carol Black*

I close my eyes and pray for light

to cast my dreams upon stone walls;

regressive, towering questions.

A story gilds by candlelight;

ink to parchment,

mind to memory.

I sink deep into pictures,

into rooms I knew and married,

deeper still into the knowing

then I awake.

Trembling.

Forgiving.

A feather.

Aware.

The shadow up the cold, stone steps

Compiler Brenda Hammon - Poems by Colleen
        Songs

was his to darken;

a separate role,

another stage,

and I the light behind his frame

to fulfill his plight to sorry,

desire unshamed,

the only way he knew how

only softer...

kinder...

real-easing me,

 innocent of his guilt-bitten ravage.

T'was not my act to polish.

I merely played the role,

that stole the show,

and drew the curtains open.

Compiler Brenda Hammon - Poems by Colleen
Songs

## Beauty Runs Deep

*For Jennifer Strachan*


Down the spiral ladder we travel,

spinning spindles as we unravel.

One step.

Two steps.

Three steps.

Four.

Look, who's knocking upon your door!


Down we go a little further,

be not afraid you're there to help her.

Five steps.

Six steps.

Seven steps.

Sacred Hearts Rising: Finding Your Wings Poems

Eight.

Real-ease your truth to consecrate.


Feel your soul return to life.

Let these steps your past to wipe.

Nine steps.

Ten Steps.

Eleven,

then

Twelve.

Bond the beauty of your greatest self.


There is no treasure that is quick to find.

We need to dig,

we need to mine.

To harvest gems

Compiler Brenda Hammon - Poems by Colleen
Songs

Sacred Hearts Rising: Finding Your Wings Poems

pray through the sluice,

without it

we

couldn't see our truth.

Compiler Brenda Hammon - Poems by Colleen
Songs

## The Music Maker

*For Kit Fraser*


Note by note

and word by word

a song gives birth.

Measured by the rhymes of living

it tortures us;

makes us pace the room,

smell the vile,

taste the glee,

simple pleasures

or travesty.

It swims into the silence of your mind.

No ears need hear it.

It walks around in your body

crazed by desire to breathe,

mollified

Compiler Brenda Hammon - Poems by Colleen
Songs

Sacred Hearts Rising: Finding Your Wings Poems

by living lullabyes,

petrified

by grunging screams.

Arias,

one by one a separate voice

drips on paper

a solo's quote.

We cannot write or sing the pleasures,

untouched by both sides

of treasures.

Without tears to smile

or sin to pray,

we have to die before we wake.

We have to feel 'fore we create.

Compiler Brenda Hammon - Poems by Colleen
Songs

## Thank You, Body.

*For Laura Lee Harrison*


Thank you body for teaching me,

for giving me a voice.

I spoke my truth,

he broke my trust

and stole my sacred choice.


I spent my life deflecting love.

His memory I would cower.

You held me still

to walk me through

each pose to regain power.


My heart still beats, my lungs expand

Sacred Hearts Rising: Finding Your Wings Poems

and breath does keep me breathing.

As every soul who wonders through

my trust again was weaving.


And when the sun came over me

I real-eyes'd the reason.

Though bruise and bones can break the soul

the shatter lets the breeze in.

Compiler Brenda Hammon - Poems by Colleen
Songs

## Dear Little Girl,

*For Laureen Nowlan-Card*


I have travelled back to the farm you see,

to search the forest to find you.

To free you.

I feel you here

skipping through the fields

picking flowers,

dancing with butterflies like Snow White in the scent.


As I've matured

I have stilled my feet,

I have kissed my wounds,

I've real-eased my fears and limiting beliefs to learn to love all parts of me

Compiler Brenda Hammon - Poems by Colleen Songs

Sacred Hearts Rising: Finding Your Wings Poems

again.

Including you.

I have come home to be

our true and wholesome self.

We were never anything but!


I've come to let you know

that I feel connected to the world now.

I've cried for you,

little girl

who lost so much of yourself here!

I've gulped the bitter aftertaste

 that only I have held us captive

 all these years.

I'm here to show you

that I am safe for you,

Compiler Brenda Hammon - Poems by Colleen
Songs

Sacred Hearts Rising: Finding Your Wings Poems

for us

to be seen and heard

laughing in the sunlight!

And as my tears of sadness turn to joy

I invite you to reunite

the playful,

imaginative,

feminine,

trusting,

innocent parts of us.

We are whole and all the wiser in the knowing.

Without the breakaway

we would not be knowing

how great the quest

Compiler Brenda Hammon - Poems by Colleen
Songs

Sacred Hearts Rising: Finding Your Wings Poems

to stand upon this once dreaded place

and welcome

each other

home.


Love,

Big Girl

Compiler Brenda Hammon - Poems by Colleen
Songs

## Monster, Monster

*For Rachel Dyer*


"Monster, Monster in the mirror,

I'm burning within flames of fear!

You choke me in this cast rod tower.

I feel the end of my breath's power."


The Monster sweeps the sterile room.

Her talons lure me to my doom.

I close my eyes, submit to die

as honey'd voice affirms the lie.


"Come closer, little pretty Girl.

I'm to protect you in this world.

Don't be afraid or judge my skin,

Sacred Hearts Rising: Finding Your Wings Poems

I offer strength from deep within."

I calm my beating fearful tears.

I run my fingers o'er the sears.

My Monster brightens from the flare.

Enchantment follows as I stare.

"Oh! Monster, Monster forgive me!

Strike my sacrificial sleep!

If I should die before I wake,

help me to lift my body's ache!"

The Monster shimmers in the glow.

I see her in the light of know.

She bares my body to the bright,

and turns the mirror t'ward my sight.

Compiler Brenda Hammon - Poems by Colleen
        Songs

Sacred Hearts Rising: Finding Your Wings Poems

"Look now, my Charge, your gift is me.

It is not who you thought you'd see.

You're more than body, more than break.

You are what your own mind creates."


My eyes adjust with living truth.

Curving ripples formed from youth.

Breasts and garden, silken skin,

dew wraps the bones I dwell within.

Compiler Brenda Hammon - Poems by Colleen
Songs

**Still**

*For Rika Harris*


She wraps her arms around her,

though so many years have passed.

Ageless is the swaddling glimpse

her body's love has cast.


The petals still remain as fresh

as when first sprinkled 'pon her.

Her scent a powdered spirit whisp,

a heart song's note to stir her.


So many came and went those days;

a brief encounter's comfort.

And slowly time has dinned the praise

Sacred Hearts Rising: Finding Your Wings Poems

of mother's loss still suffered.

Phones run cold and flowers dry,

the silence lends denial,

that mother's love diminishes

a sealed and lost time capsule.

The span between a mother's grief

and peace within the pleasure,

is vast like universal wings

from memories she still treasures.

So fill that void and speak her name

when in her Mother's presence!

Though we can't see her flitter 'bout

she still can feel her essence...

Compiler Brenda Hammon - Poems by Colleen
Songs

## Trust the Flight

*For Sheryl Rist*

I trust. I ache.

Climb up to break.

I reach. I fall.

Go away! Stand tall!

I am that brave.

I am that child.

Who stopped the fate

of a girl's green mile.

"It is perfect.

It's okay.

I am no

longer afraid

to fly."


Breathe in, breathe out.

Sacred Hearts Rising: Finding Your Wings Poems

Love in, love out.

I feel. Become.

I sing. I hum.

I walk this walk,

open the cage.

I build a fence

to guard with sage.

"It is perfect.

It's okay.

I am no

longer afraid

to fly."


I stand. I crawl.

Feel through it all.

The dark brings light.

The blind brings sight.

I hear birds sing.

Compiler Brenda Hammon - Poems by Colleen
Songs

Sacred Hearts Rising: Finding Your Wings Poems

I set my wings.
By water's edge
a fledgling's pledge:

"It is perfect.
It's okay.
There is no fear
when you trust
the flight."

Compiler Brenda Hammon - Poems by Colleen
Songs

## More For Me (Morphine)

*For Sue Ferreira*

Endorphins ran through me like bright shooting morphine

when body let go of brain.

Thirty three years end a life with another awakened my memory again.


What, when and where would I be without living this life I had settled so long?

How could I help all the others left wondering

their fate once their present is gone?


How could I help when I'm here in the struggle

and seeing the need for myself?

But who else could lead it than one who had lived it

so I dusted my doubts off the shelf.

Sacred Hearts Rising: Finding Your Wings Poems

Us women live longer and longer by living and
do so by giving so much.

We forget our own weakness and strengths
when we need them,

dependence can harbour our touch.


So I set my goals higher than I ever desired

and created a path lit to tread;

a stepping stone walkway to bring us our some
day

of wisdom and wealthy and fed.


And I tell my own story to serve all the worries

 in order to say "It can be!"

It just take some planning and time's
understanding

to guilt-free a life more for me.

Compiler Brenda Hammon - Poems by Colleen
Songs

## Scars

*For Tracy Childs*

They hide within your memory.
They linger on your skin.
They mark your steps through history.
They mimic story's whim.

They harbour you on foggy nights.
They cast a shadow's light.
They burn when darkness settles in.
They whimper through the fright.

And when you run your fingers
over every singing seam,
they silence with your feather's touch
but inside they still scream.

Compiler Brenda Hammon - Poems by Colleen
Songs

Sacred Hearts Rising: Finding Your Wings Poems

All you can do it kiss them
with a listening tender ear.
Kiss them without wondering why
their only love is fear.

Show them life is normal when
we have to jump the curb.
The bumps are just reminders
that forewarn our path to swerve.

And without jerks and jolts through life
we wouldn't heart a beat.
The healing comes to surface
when we live, love, learn, repeat.

Compiler Brenda Hammon - Poems by Colleen
Songs

## Paula,

*For Wendy Walsh*

He stole from you.
You stole from me.
Who robbed him his innocence
holds the master key.
I fled what felt wrong,
left you in the deep,
I wish I had wakened you
out of the sleep.

It's taken me years
to reopen this page;
a secret kept hidden
within the shame cage.
Until I revealed,
and I shared

71

Sacred Hearts Rising: Finding Your Wings Poems

and admitted
that you were a victim,
our guilt I acquitted!

I thank God we're just body,
our soul's b'long to Him.
The ashes will shed us
of broken trust's skin.
And no matter the breaker
it's their shameful sin.
We aren't what is done
we're the beauty within.

Compiler Brenda Hammon - Poems by Colleen
Songs

## *Colleen Songs*

Colleen Songs is a Canadian Singer-Songwriter who has been spreading her message of using your gifts and talents to lead you to the fulfillment of your wildest dreams.

She began singing and writing when she was 14 and used her talent to take her through adolescence, romance, heartache, back to love, motherhood, wellness, trauma, and the loss of a loved one with mental illness.

She has fought MS for the past 21 years and has recently begun singing once again following a car accident that caused her to have emergency neck surgery, leaving her more afraid of losing her voice than afraid of the surgery.

Currently, Colleen is in the midst of producing her second album, "This Life," with BCCMA and CCMA Award Winning Producer, Tom McKillip. She is publishing her memoir, "INHALE," with Tellwell Publishing Canada, based on the life of a caregiver of a loved one with mental illness, where the gift of song-writing kept the caregiver alive and dreaming her dream.

Her music and speaking journey has brought her as far as Nashville's Canadian Country Music Hall Of Fame, to the stages of eWomen Network, Women Embracing

Sacred Hearts Rising: Finding Your Wings Poems

Brilliance, Dreams Take Flight, Kamp Kiwanis, WomenTalk, Blue-Friday, and most recently Gems for Gems, and Sacred Hearts Rising!

With her goal to support anyone's dream of any gender, age, or gift-ability (NOT dis-ability), please welcome Colleen Songs as she inspires the priceless gems within each of us called Gifts and Talents.
And remember..."Dreams Never Expire!" xo Colleen Songs
**www.colleensongs.com**
**www.facebook.com/ColleenSongs**
**www.twitter.com/ColleenSongs**
**https://www.instagram.com/collee**
**nsongsca**

Compiler Brenda Hammon - Poems by Colleen Songs

Sacred Hearts Rising: Finding Your Wings Poems

*Brenda Hammon*

International Inspirational and Motivational Speaker, Entrepreneur, Philanthropist, International Best Selling Author, International Award Winning Writer and equestrian Brenda Hammon kicks down the walls of silence surrounding abuse.

Brenda is a catalyst for finding 'Your' happy and has been called an 'Adversity'

Compiler Brenda Hammon - Poems by Colleen Songs

Expert and has shared her experience on many stages.

Brenda is a storyteller of true life events that everybody is afraid to talk about openly, but want to read about.

Brenda is the CEO and founder of ***Sacred Hearts Rising***, http://www.sacredheartsrising.

In denial of the ways abuse had permeated her life for forty years, Brenda suffered in silence and isolation, until finally taking a stand and dealing with her past. Known for her integrity, courage, and directness, Brenda now works to show others who have been abused that they too have a voice and can take back control of their lives. Brenda takes pride in breaking the cycle of abuse in her own family and speaking out loud to prevent the suffering of other children.

Not one to shy away from a challenge, Brenda decided to break the

77

cycle of silence around topics that are not talked about openly in our society.

Brenda makes her home with her husband Bud on their small farm outside of Alberta Beach, Alberta.

**www.brendahammon.com**

**www.sacredheartsrising.com**

**www.facebook.com/brenda.hammon.9**

**linkedin.com/in/brenda-hammon-b5431a27**

**Twitter@BrendaHammon**

**Instagram BrendaHammon**

Sacred Hearts Rising: Finding Your Wings Poems

Other books by complier/author:

I can't hear the birds anymore

I AM: Kicking Down the Walls of Silence

Hear Me: No Longer Silent

Sacred Hearts Rising: Breaking the Silence One
       Story at A Time

Sacred Hearts Rising Sisterhood Poems Book I

Sacred Hearts Rising: Finding Your Wings

Compiler Brenda Hammon - Poems by Colleen
Songs